MELISSA F. FIELDS

FEARLESS IN HIGH HEELS
"180 Turning Points Toward Fearless Living"

**A lexicon of quotes for women who are ready
to tread on serpents and scorpions,
step into new assignments,
walk in His will,
step up to their Goliath challenges,
and take leaps of faith toward their destiny …
in their most fashionable kitten, pumps, or stiletto heels.**

FEARLESS IN HIGH HEELS

MELISSA F. FIELDS

FEARLESS IN HIGH HEELS
"180 Turning Points Toward Fearless Living"

MELISSA F. FIELDS

MELISSA F. FIELDS

FEARLESS IN HIGH HEELS
180 Turning Points Toward Fearless Living

WWW.FEARLESSINHIGHEELS.COM

FEARLESS IN HIGH HEELS
"180 Turning Points Toward Fearless Living"

ACKNOWLEDGEMENTS

My LORD and Savior, Jesus Christ -- I adore You! Your presence has been a mainstay during this writing process. I value Your encouragement and next-step directives. Thank You for freeing me from the spirit of fear. Because of You, I am "Fearless In High Heels."

My Husband, Pastor, Bishop, and Friend, W. Michael Fields -- Your encouragement has been consistent. I value your willingness to read the first manuscript. You have emboldened me throughout this writing assignment. You absolutely have contributed to my being, "Fearless In High Heels."

My Parents, Dorothy J. Green and Phillip Green, Jr --Your nurturing, teaching, and guidance have assisted me in becoming the woman of God that I am. Because of you, I am "Fearless In High Heels."

My Sister, Monique Johnson --Your make-it-happen attitude, protection, long talks, and generous nature have nurtured me to be "Fearless In High Heels."

DEDICATION

To the fabulous women who are the "Fearless In High Heels" community, for pushing me to step livelier in my high heels.

INTRODUCTION

Fear has a cunning voice, injecting its corroded thought systems within women. This little book exposes the shrewd antics of fear. There is no depth to which fear will not go, to impede the progress of God's women. In your hands is a plethora of nuggets of knowledge, winning wisdom, and impeccable inspiration to get you moving confidently in your most fashionable and high-power heels.

This is a lexicon of quotes for women who are ready to tread on serpents and scorpions, step into new assignments, walk in His will, step up to their Goliath challenges, and take leaps of faith toward their destiny ... in their most fashionable kitten, pumps, or stiletto heels. The quotes are from the: Bible, reference books, and personal experience. These bite-size quotes will have you walking into the boardroom, chatting with big wigs, sauntering into the presentation, and stepping up to the podium with a confidence that has bound every fearful whisper.

This book of quotes presents women with 180 turning points. It supplies women with quantifiable quotes for pivoting from fear into the direction of bold living for 180 days. If a woman physically turns 180-degrees, she will perform a complete turnaround -- pointing her entire body in the opposite direction. A fearless woman pivots flawlessly in her high heels when the spirit of fear approaches. She does not move cowardly in the opposite direction. She moves purposefully toward faith and her divine destiny. She is "Fearless In High Heels."

Day 1 to Day 180 features a fear-smashing quote. According to Merriam-Webster Dictionary, *"fear is defined as an unpleasant often strong emotion caused by anticipation or an awareness of danger."* There is a natural fear, sinful fear, and religious fear. Fear is an instinctive part of us naturally, it is a part of our sin nature, and we should fear (worship) God. This book primarily looks at dealing with reflex and sinful fears. Whether you are full of faith, have fizzling faith, or are fixing frazzled faith, each day will provide faith-boosting content which demolishes the spirit of fear. Each quote offers an opportunity to whisper a prayer that God would release you from every fear that is forbidding you to fulfill your Kingdom assignments.

So, ladies, pull out your favorite heels and let's get ready to step into these God-ordained assignments, walk in His will, and saunter outside of old comfort zones.

PREFACE

"Fear Not, Daughter" is a message from God to His people, found in the gospel of John 12:15. God wants His Daughter, Israel, to know that He is coming. He wants to conquer the fears of His people. He comes to quiet all our fears. "Fearless In High Heels" is about hearing the voice of God say, "Don't be afraid, Daughter! I am with you. I am here."

Fear can wear the disguise of procrastination, second-guessing, excuse making, feelings of dread or anxiety, avoiding events, and irrational inner questions. In the midst of each deceptive tactic, God says, "Fear Not, Daughter!"

In addition to hearing God's fear-calming voice, "Fearless In High Heels" will be the voice of a sister-friend. A feminine voice that says to you, "Girl, never mind that thought! Honey, put on your favorite heels and let's walk fearlessly!"

Melissa F. Fields is our high-heel coach. Creating content to help women thrive in their life roles and goals. This ministry provides inspiration for women to be effective in their home life, the marketplace, the workplace and in the church. She is "Fearless In High Heels."

EPIGRAPH

Fear not, daughter of Zion: behold,
thy King cometh, sitting on an ass's colt.
John 12:15

FEARLESS IN HIGH HEELS
"180 Turning Points Toward Fearless Living"

Day 1
FEARLESS IN HIGH HEELS
180 Turning Points Toward Fearless Living

When fear comes
holler to the top of your lungs,
"JEEEEEESUUUUUUS!"

Day 2
FEARLESS IN HIGH HEELS
180 Turning Points Toward Fearless Living

Fear will cause you to flounder feverishly,
fixate on the negative, and fluctuate
between bad and worst-case scenarios.

Fearless women ask God to do Herculean,
impossible, and miraculous things
which will bring God maximum glory.

A fearless mindset does not entice a
woman to act recklessly.
A fearless woman blends the
fear-not mindset with sound wisdom
and an intense faith in God.

Sometimes an authentic fearless
woman sees herself as a young girl,
completely unphased, skipping along,
holding her father's hand, while
crossing a dangerous intersection.
She has no reason to fear!

A fearless woman turns
confining fears into liberating prayers.

Fear will ferociously attack faith.

Day 8
FEARLESS IN HIGH HEELS
180 Turning Points Toward Fearless Living

When your faith gets big enough
it will begin to viciously attack
the most polarizing fears.

Faith is like a highly skilled sniper ... it will win
the battle against the fear of rejection,
fear of failure, fear of launching out into
the deep, and the fear of man.

Fear will have you ruminating on the fact
that you are about to be exposed
and shamed when the truth is you
are mere seconds away from
being radically blessed!

Fear may take on the form of low
self-esteem, negative inner chatter,
or self-doubt. The purpose? To stare
you down and dare you to take one
step further toward your purpose.

Fear will throw you a pity party and
will refuse to stop playing the blues songs,
will keep feeding your feelings
with buckets of ice cream and pounds of chocolate,
and will continue to
lull you off to sleep for
elongated-depressive naps.

Fear is like quicksand; it is not a firm
foundation on which stand.

You can break the bars and unlock the doors
to the prison of fear. How? Just tell yourself the polar
opposite of what fear has been telling you.

Every time fear approaches you
it is an opportunity to make a 180-degree turn.

Fear has a voice! Do not listen to the
inflection, tone, or words spoken by fear.

One place where you will hear "Fear Not!" resoundingly clear is in the prayer room.

Look yourself in the mirror! Release the fear of exposure and tell yourself the whole truth about who you are. Then ask God to help you speak faith to the little girl in you.

Day 19
FEARLESS IN HIGH HEELS
180 Turning Points Toward Fearless Living

If you let fear run at breakneck speed through
your life you will be a mere shell of the
woman God designed you to be.

Day 20
FEARLESS IN HIGH HEELS
180 Turning Points Toward Fearless Living

Fear is a weapon of mass destruction,
unleashed from the pit of hell
to sabotage your whole life.

Fear will destroy your peace of mind,
your closest relationships,
and zap you of your spiritual strength.

Fear is a ruthless thief.

Fear will tell you the bold lie that God is
not El Shaddai -- the almighty God --
who is able to do absolutely anything.

Day 24
FEARLESS IN HIGH HEELS
180 Turning Points Toward Fearless Living

Fear will constantly invite its good girlfriends over:
Confused Cora, Weak Wanda, and Antagonizing Ann …
here they all come to sit on your sofa.
Sis, you do not have to entertain any of them!

Fearless women trust God in the sunshine,
in the rain, and in the storm.

The reassuring voice of faith will hush the
whispers of the taunting voice of fear.

Day 27
FEARLESS IN HIGH HEELS
180 Turning Points Toward Fearless Living

Fear has a way of causing you to shake in your boots because of what you do see. Fear also has a knack for causing you to shake in your stilettos over what you do not see.

Day 28
FEARLESS IN HIGH HEELS
180 Turning Points Toward Fearless Living

Sis, you have to choose every single day ....
Fear or Faith! You do get to decide.

God says, "Fear Not!"
Now what are you going to do?

While fear is whispering innuendo in your ear
you whisper a fear-smashing prayer
and then move forward in faith.

Day 31
FEARLESS IN HIGH HEELS
180 Turning Points Toward Fearless Living

The spirit of fear does not come from God.

The fear which speaks to you has an
assignment to fulfill.

Fear has cousins: anxiety, worry, dread, and excessive
questioning. And they all love to host their Family Reunion in
your mind.

Make sure your faith is stronger than the fears trying to halt your frontward motion.

Heaven declared the words, "Fear Not!" to Abram, Hagar, Daniel, Mary, Peter, and other Bible patriarchs. He is still speaking today, "Fear Not!"

Fear feels powerful,
but its power is deceptive.

The aim of fear is to slow your gait, cause an
unsteady pace, and completely maim
your forward momentum.

Fear is a fact of life!

Fear of Failure
Fear of Loss
Fear of Criticism
Fear of Exposure
Fear of Rejection
Fear of the Unknown
None of them come from God!

Day 40
FEARLESS IN HIGH HEELS
180 Turning Points Toward Fearless Living

Several times in the Word, God says:
"Fear Not, I am ..."

Day 41
FEARLESS IN HIGH HEELS
180 Turning Points Toward Fearless Living

Fear will wear down fervor and cause
you to move from possessing a fiery passion
to aimlessly walking with a lifeless disinterest.

Say this, "I Will Not Fear!"

Practical Tip: Oils which calm fear and anxiety are
Bergamot orange, Chamomile,
Clary sage, Lavender, Lemon, Neroli,
Peppermint, Rose, Fennel, and Jasmine.

If your fear is beyond situational,
please consider speaking with your physician.

Day 44
FEARLESS IN HIGH HEELS
180 Turning Points Toward Fearless Living

Say this out loud, "God will take care of me!"

Day 45
FEARLESS IN HIGH HEELS
180 Turning Points Toward Fearless Living

John the Revelator was incarcerated on an island when He heard the voice of God, "Fear Not!"

Day 46
FEARLESS IN HIGH HEELS
180 Turning Points Toward Fearless Living

A fearless woman refuses to permit fear to be the impetus of any of her decision making.

Say this out loud and with courage,
"I Will Fear NOOOOOOOO Evil!"

Out Loud … Remind Fear Who You Are!

I am loved.
I am forgiven.
I am adopted of God.
I am born of God.
I am redeemed.
I am rescued.
I am chosen.
I am accepted.

Day 49
FEARLESS IN HIGH HEELS
180 Turning Points Toward Fearless Living

When God gives you a Kingdom assignment
it will tower over you and intimidate you.
Trust me ... soon you will also hear God say,
"Fear Not!"

Day 50
FEARLESS IN HIGH HEELS
180 Turning Points Toward Fearless Living

Fear will have your eyes bulging and your
heart racing over what God already told
you He was going to handle.

Fear will ask you over
and over
and over again,
"Did you hear what I said?"

Day 52
FEARLESS IN HIGH HEELS
180 Turning Points Toward Fearless Living

The feeling of fear is like
tripping a silent alarm.
When you feel fear
sound the alarm because great things
are ahead if you just push past fear.

If you are not careful, you will look at a portrait of yourself for a long period of time before you look down and see the Artist's Signature on the painting -- Signed, *Fear*.

When fear grabs you by both shoulders and tries to make eye contact with you, look up and focus your mind on who God is.

Fear will tempt you to lock your
eyes on the thing you fear most.

It is not beneath fear to swindle
its way into your dreams.

Day 57
FEARLESS IN HIGH HEELS
180 Turning Points Toward Fearless Living

Point to yourself and say,
"I have no reason to fear!"

Day 58
FEARLESS IN HIGH HEELS
180 Turning Points Toward Fearless Living

Excuses are kinsfolk to fear!

Say this out loud, **"Yea, though
I walk through the valley of the shadow of death, I will fear
no evil: for thou art with me; thy rod and thy staff they
comfort me."** Psalm 23:4

Let fear hear you say this,
"I am a woman of COURAGE!"

C = Calm
O = Oil Bearing
U = Unafraid
R = Renowned
A = Accomplished
G = Genuine and
E = Empowered

Boldly say, **"The Lord *is* my helper, and I will not fear what man shall do unto me."** Hebrews 13:6

Thoughts of fear will prey hardest
when you are trying to
pray the hardest.

If you pray once and the fearful situation
is not completely resolved, pray again,
and again, and again!

Definition:
Bold is defined as "fearless before danger
showing or requiring a fearless daring spirit."
Merriam Webster

A fearless woman knows the precise
moment when she must say to one of
the members of her tribe, "Fear Not!"
No way, no fear over here.

Say this, "I am a FEARLESS woman!"

F = Feminine
E = Edgy
A = Amazing
R = Real
L = Loving
E = Enterprising
S = Stunning and so
S = Stylish

Fear will tell you a good, dramatic, action-packed and suspenseful story with a tragic ending.

What it means to be fearless!
Designing a fearless life does not mean
all your fears will disappear.
Designing a fearless life means
you boldly move
despite fear until you overcome.

Scripture & Biblical Confession

**"He shall not be afraid of evil tidings:
his heart is fixed, trusting in the LORD."**
Psalm 112:7

No matter what the enemy says
I will look towards heaven and say,
"LORD, I love you and I trust you completely."

Vocalize this: "I am a BOLD woman of The King!"

B = Brilliant
O = Overflowing
L = Lady-Like and
D = Daring

God's fearless woman is a divine mix of
bravery, compassion, kindness, humility,
gentleness, wisdom, patience, and business-savvy.

God's fearless woman of prayer expects sudden shifts,
prepares for waves of favor,
and anticipates doors swinging wide open.

Look yourself in the mirror and say,
"I am a BRAVE woman of God!"

B = Brilliant
R = Resilient
A = Adventurous
V = Virtuous and
E = Effervescent

Sometimes fear moves quickly,
bombarding and scattering
every rational thought.

Fill In The Blank

The Lord is with me in the elevator.
The Lord is with me in the car.
The Lord is with me in a plane.
The Lord is with me in a ship.
The Lord is with me in _____.

Day 76
FEARLESS IN HIGH HEELS
180 Turning Points Toward Fearless Living

An opposite of fear is rest.
REST! REST! REST! REST!

God has already given you the victory over fear.

Fear will either push you closer to or pull
you further away from God.

Investigate your fears in the Word and prayer.

Just like He spoke to the winds and the waves
He speaks to you in the midst of
frantic fear,
waves of worry, and
abyssal anxiety ….
"Peace, be still!"

Day 81

Say this out loud:
"I am going to rebuke the spirit of fear!"

Speak this into the atmosphere:
"I WILL NOT FEAR."

Battle Strategy Against Fear

"(For the weapons of our warfare are not carnal, but mighty through God to the pulling down of strong holds;) Casting down imaginations, and every high thing that exalteth itself against the knowledge of God, and bringing into captivity every thought to the obedience of Christ..."
2 Corinthians 10:4-5

Day 84
FEARLESS IN HIGH HEELS
180 Turning Points Toward Fearless Living

Repeat what the Psalmist verbalized, out loud:
**"I will not be afraid of ten thousands of people,
that have set themselves against
me round about."** Psalm 3:6

You must be willing to fight fear!

Introduce your fears to the God of the universe.

Day 87
FEARLESS IN HIGH HEELS
180 Turning Points Toward Fearless Living

Refuse to entertain fearful thoughts.

Day 88
FEARLESS IN HIGH HEELS
180 Turning Points Toward Fearless Living

Turn a deaf ear to fearful promptings.

Trust the Word, not the destructive
suggestions that fear will introduce.

Refuse to follow the tragically fatal plot that fear wants to play
out in your mind.

Do not allow fearful thoughts to take center stage.

Day 92
FEARLESS IN HIGH HEELS
180 Turning Points Toward Fearless Living

God repeatedly said in His Word, "Be strong!"

Day 93
FEARLESS IN HIGH HEELS
180 Turning Points Toward Fearless Living

Fear will place you in a headlock
and clamp down on your head like a vice.

Fear will attempt to isolate you from others.

A symptom of fear is avoidance.

A courageous woman vehemently resists fear
by using the Name, the blood,
and the authority of Jesus Christ.

Be fearless in advancing
heaven's agenda in the earth.

A fearless woman knows that God is at
the helm during thunderstorms,
typhoons, and tsunamis.

Do not let fear zip your lips shut!
Open your mouth and declare,
confess, and proclaim God's Word …
fearlessly.

God's fearless woman knows the importance
of becoming comfortable with dealing with the fear of man.
She remembers the Word of The Lord,
**"Thou shalt not be affrighted at them: for the Lord thy God is
among you, a mighty God and terrible."**
Deuteronomy 7:21

The fear of man includes attempting
to avoid the sneers of gossiping lips,
whispering snickers, and critical feedback.

Definition:
Confident is defined as "full of conviction,
certain, having or showing assurance."
Merriam Webster

Kick the fear of man's disapproval to the curb
and fulfill God's confirmed Word in your life.

A fearless woman is confident and kind
even under tyrannical leadership.

A fearless woman graciously mixes submission
and honor into each of her relationships.

Fear has a convincing voice, but it is still lying.

Fear will cause you to beat yourself up until
you are completely black and blue.

Speak this into the atmosphere:
**"The LORD is on my side;
I will not fear: what can man do unto me?"**
Psalm 118:6

Just so we are clear,
if you say "yes" to a commitment
when God clearly told you to say, "no"
…. you could be struggling with the fear of man.

A fearless woman is completely convinced
that man can-not do
anything to her from which God can not
quickly deliver her. She refuses to bow to
the commands of the fear of man.

Replay, God's Word over in your mind:
"Have not I commanded thee? Be strong and of a good courage; be not afraid, neither be thou dismayed: for the Lord thy God is with thee whithersoever thou goest."
Joshua 1:9

Day 112
FEARLESS IN HIGH HEELS
180 Turning Points Toward Fearless Living

Sis, look yourself in the mirror and say,
**"Ye shall not fear them: for the Lord your
God He shall fight for you."**
Deuteronomy 3:22

Day 113
FEARLESS IN HIGH HEELS
180 Turning Points Toward Fearless Living

Excessive and clingy neediness and
the fear of being alone
is fear that must be submitted to God.

Push the fear of man away from you, Sis!
Open your mouth and declare,
**"What time I am afraid, I will trust in thee.
In God I will praise his word, in God I have
put my trust; I will not fear what flesh
can do unto me."**
Psalm 56:3-4

Personalize This Scripture
Place Your name where Daniel's name is:

**"Fear not, Daniel: for from the first day
that thou didst set thine heart to understand,
and to chasten thyself before thy God,
thy words were heard, and I am come
for thy words.** Daniel 10:12

You do not have to be a slave to fear!

A vicious cycle of negative thinking could offer an entry point for the spirit of fear.

Day 118
FEARLESS IN HIGH HEELS
180 Turning Points Toward Fearless Living

The Lord gave these words of comfort
to Israel and He consoles you,
with His words, **"Fear ... not; for I am
with thee: be not dismayed; for I am thy God:
I will strengthen thee; yea, I will help thee;
yea, I will uphold thee with the
right hand of my righteousness."**
Isaiah 41:10

Although avoiding conflict alleviates anxiety
in the short term, in the long term
it perpetuates the fear that you can not
handle situations involving conflict.
You cannot cower to the fear of conflict.

His voice shatters our doubts
with the two words "Fear Not!"

The fear of man will try to paralyze you
when you should move forward in the Spirit,
and muzzle you when
you should boldly speak.

When fears are driving you into a dark hole ...
hear heaven say, "Fear Not!"

At a crossroads in your life ... hear God say,
"Fear Not!"

When faith seems the lowest and the situation seems the
bleakest, hear heaven say,
"Fear Not!"

It is when the image of failure is standing tallest
that you need to hear heaven declare,
"Fear Not!"

Shadrach, Meshach, and Abednego
would tell you,
"Don't fear the fiery furnace!"

Speak this in the Earth realm:
"I am a CONFIDENT woman!"

C = Centered
O = Optimistic
N = Necessary
F = Far-Reaching
I = Illuminated a
D = Designer's Original
E = Established
N = Notable and
T = Tenacious

Definition:
Courage is defined as "mental or moral strength to venture, persevere, and withstand danger, fear, or difficulty."

Merriam Webster

Live above anxiety and fear.

Ambivalence can leave footprints in
the sand that lead directly to the
den of the spirit of fear.

Proverbs 18:21 says, **"A man's gift maketh
room for him, and bringeth him before great men."**
Sis, when you get before great men (and you will),
here is one piece of advice: "Fear Not!"

Excessive "what ifs" can walk
you directly into the dark cave of fear.

Fear will cause you to make false
Prophecy -- speaking forth fearful and
false projections concerning your future.

Definition:

Fear is defined as "a distressing emotion
aroused by impending danger, evil, pain, etc.,
whether the threat is real or imagined; the
feeling or condition of being afraid."

Dictionary.com

Talk with The Lord about the fear
that is confronting you. Get His thoughts
on whether it is a valid
concern or excessive worry.

Command antagonizing fear
to leave you alone!

Adam and Eve will tell you,
"Fear will give you the impulse
to hide from the voice and presence of God."

**Fear is a bully!
It will push and shove
you away from your
God-ordained destiny.**

When you really get free of fear
you will find yourself whispering,
"Yes, LORD!"

Irrational fear can be debilitating!

Fear will put on a disguise and approach you.
Fear may show up masked as distraction or
even procrastination. Do not be tricked!
It is still fear.

Day 139
FEARLESS IN HIGH HEELS
180 Turning Points Toward Fearless Living

Perfectionism is a mask that fear wears.
Perfectionism will impede you from
taking on Kingdom assignments.

The fear of failure will slowly erode
every ounce of your confidence.

David spoke into the life of his son,
Solomon telling Solomon that God
had foreordained that Solomon
would build God's House. David settled
any fear of failure within Solomon:
**"Then shalt thou prosper, if thou
takest heed to fulfil the statutes
and judgments which the
LORD charges Moses with
concerning Israel: be strong,
and of good courage dread not,
nor be dismayed."**
II Chronicles 22:13

Daniel would tell you with confidence, "Do not fear the lion's den."

A woman who is fearless in high heels does feel fear; she just kicks irrational fear to the curb and keeps walking forward in her Kingdom purpose.

**When God gives you a
kingdom-assignment,
fear will always put in its two cents.**

**Fear will get you in the middle of a terrifying situation
and say, "Now, RUN!"
Faith will get you in the middle of the same terrifying situation
and say, "Believe God .. Fear Not!"**

Day 146
FEARLESS IN HIGH HEELS
180 Turning Points Toward Fearless Living

Say this to fear,
"Shhhhhhhhhhhhhhhhhhhhhhhhhh!"

God acknowledges that fear will come.
How do you know?
He says, "Fear Not!"
several times throughout The Bible.

"Fear Not!"
"Fear Not!"
"Fear Not!"
"Fear Not!"
"Fear Not!"

Favor will usher you into large rooms with highly influential people. When you get into the room with the brand influencers, financial gurus, and CEO professionals, "Do Not Fear!"

If you are afraid of rejection, humiliating yourself, or ending up alone despite your best efforts, the fear of abandonment may be what the enemy is attempting to use against you.

If your worst nightmares paint visions of you
performing assignments inadequately, being unable to
financially support your family,
or your child not living up to your
highest dreams, it is possible
you are caught in the snare of the fear of failure.

A fearless woman strives to complete God's assignments with excellence not perfection.
There is a huge difference!

Courage is the opposite of fear;
it is the ability to face danger without fear.

The fear of man includes
superiors, peers, and subordinates.
**"By faith he forsook Egypt, not fearing the
wrath of the king: for he endured, as
seeing him wo is invisible."**
Hebrews 11:27

Parental fears must be given to God.
**"By faith Moses, when he was born,
was hid three months of his parents,
because they saw he was a proper
child; and they were not afraid
of the king's commandment."**
Hebrews 11:23

**"Therefore will not we fear, though the earth
be removed, and though the mountains be carried
into the midst of the sea."** Psalm 46:2

The fear of commitment whispers,
"They don't love you! People are so deceptive.
If you join that team they are going to ridicule you.
He is going to hurt me."
Confront every type of fear
which attempts to harass you!

Fear will chat all day long if you permit it.

Day 158
FEARLESS IN HIGH HEELS
180 Turning Points Toward Fearless Living

Some days you need to glare at the fear of man and ask a couple of questions: **"The Lord is my light and my salvation; WHOM SHALL I FEAR? the Lord is the strength of my life; OF WHOM SHALL I BE AFRAID?"**
Psalm 27:1

God is about to bring you into a room of high prestige. When you cross the threshold, encourage yourself with these words ... "Fear Not!"

When the mission calls for it,
snipers dismantle and dishearten
the enemy with well-placed rifle shots.
Just like faith. Faith will release arrows
of impenetrable confidence which will pierce
doubt, deflate fearful thoughts,
and incapacitate the fear of failure.

Fear absolutely hates it when
a woman has a crystal clear
view of who her God is.

Fear will insist that you
crop, clip, retouch, and filter
the original picture God gave you.

Day 163
FEARLESS IN HIGH HEELS
180 Turning Points Toward Fearless Living

A woman who is prepared for the next
level can expect surprising phone calls
from high-level movers and shakers.
When you get the call (and you will),
"Fear Not!"

Fear has a knack for multiplying itself.
Fear, when entertained, births more fear!

Ruminating on painful flashbacks --
where you are recalling
all of the feelings of hopelessness, violation,
and humiliation -- can lead to the
fear of commitment.

If you are continually sabotaging friendships/relationships and you dodge sharing your feelings, ideas, and information in a close emotional or physical relationship, you may be struggling with the fear of intimacy.

The enemy continually will use the fear of death against
you. When you feel the fear of crossing
bridges or the anxiety of going through
tunnels, say this: **"Yea, though I walk through
the valley of the shadow of death, I will
fear no evil: for thou art with me; thy rod
and thy staff they comfort me."**
Psalm 23:4

Day 168
FEARLESS IN HIGH HEELS
180 Turning Points Toward Fearless Living

Declare this:
**"The LORD is my light and my salvation;
whom shall I fear? the LORD is the
strength of my life; of whom shall
I be afraid?"** Psalm 27:1

Day 169
FEARLESS IN HIGH HEELS
180 Turning Points Toward Fearless Living

Say this: "God is with me. Right now,
He is with me. His presence surrounds me.
He is here to protect me."

I Am Not TIMID

T - Threatened
I - Insecure
M - Misguided
I - Immobilized or
D - Dejected.

A fearless inward response to a request for
you to: pray publicly, speak publicly, share
a testimony, handle a high-level assignment,
step up to take on a leading lady role, and
creative spiritual tasks ... should be ...
**"I can do all things through Christ
which strengtheneth me."**
Philippians 4:13

When you're praying and waiting, remember what the angel told Daniel: **"Fear not, Daniel: for from the first day that thou didst set thine heart to understand, and to chasten thyself before thy God, thy words were heard, and I am come for thy words."** Daniel 10:12

Practical Tip: Vitamins A, B-Complex, C, and D, Omega-3 Fatty Acids, and Magnesium may be helpful vitamins in managing anxiety.

Severe anxiety should be discussed with a primary care physician. This information should not be used in place of the advice of your physician or other qualified healthcare providers.

Oh, what wonderful words
precede and proceed a
"Fear Not!" message
from heaven.

"… the righteous are bold as a lion."
Proverbs 28:1

Fear will insinuate the uninterrupted
continuation of generational issues
(financial, physical, mental, and emotional).
Do not believe fear for a millisecond.

Day 177
FEARLESS IN HIGH HEELS
180 Turning Points Toward Fearless Living

Pssssssssst, if you are a control freak,
you do realize that is really fear
in an elaborate disguise?

Do not allow fear to nestle down in your ear!

It is permissible to articulate that you are afraid;
but, it is never ok to succumb to fear.

God's Fearless Woman is LIONHEARTED.
She is …

L = Lovely
I = Illuminated
O = Optimistic
N = Noteworthy
H = High-Class
E = Essential
A = Accomplished
R = Riveting
T = Tenacious
E = Enterprising and
D = Decisive

FEARLESS IN HIGH HEELS
"180 Turning Points Toward Fearless Living"

FEARLESS IN HIGH HEELS
"180 Turning Points Toward Fearless Living"

Made in United States
North Haven, CT
31 July 2022

22038591R00096